Lining Up

Books by Richard Howard

Poetry

LINING UP *1983*

MISGIVINGS *1979*

FELLOW FEELINGS *1976*

TWO-PART INVENTIONS *1974*

FINDINGS *1971*

UNTITLED SUBJECTS *1969*

THE DAMAGES *1967*

QUANTITIES *1962*

Criticism

ALONE WITH AMERICA *1969*

PREFERENCES *1974*

LINING UP

Poems *by* **Richard Howard**

New York Atheneum 1984

The poems have been previously published as follows:

LINING UP   *(Grand Street)*
ON HEARING YOUR LOVER   *(New Republic)*
EUGÈNE DELACROIX   *(Salmagundi)*
JEAN-FRANÇOIS MILLET   *(Salmagundi)*
JEAN-BAPTISTE CAMILLE COROT   *(Raritan Review)*
GIUSEPPE VERDI   *(The Nation)*
HECTOR BERLIOZ   *(Raritan Review)*
GÉRARD DE NERVAL   *(Raritan Review)*
ANATOLE FRANCE   *(The Nation)*
ON LATELY LOOKING INTO CHAPMAN'S JANE AUSTEN   *(Grand Street)*
CARRION (CONTINUED)   *(Grand Street)*
HOMAGE   *(University of Pennsylvania Press)*
IMPERSONATIONS   *(Grand Street)*
AT THE MONUMENT TO PIERRE LOUYS   *(The Nation)*
ATTIC RED-FIGURE CALYX   *(Yale Review)*
ITHACA: THE PALACE AT FOUR A.M.   *(Grand Street)*
CYGNUS CYGNUS TO LEDA   *(Vanity Fair)*
NARCISSUS EXPLAINS   *(Grand Street)*

Published simultaneously in Canada by McClelland and Stewart Ltd
Library of Congress catalog card number 83–45121
ISBN   *0–689–11420–6 (clothbound)*
     0–689–11421–4 (paperback)
Composition by Heritage Printers, Inc., Charlotte, North Carolina
Manufactured by Fairfield Graphics, Fairfield, Pennsylvania
Designed by Harry Ford
First Edition

And the painter has brooded on them
and brought forth another showing.
He has made details over,
made them retrace their steps and correct
their errors, repent their sins
and transfigure all the past,
altering what had been done
to what never was. . .

I

I I   *Homage to Nadar (II)*

I I I

I V   *Hellenistics*

V

(I)

Lining Up

Pasadena: the museum vestibule

Better stay where we are: here at least
we have, however odd, what passes
    for a roof over our heads,
and even if the walls are nothing
more than glass, they will be nothing less;
    how else take in so clearly
these citizens coming upon us
in radiant raiment, the motley
    of Southern California?
Where else but in Eden could we find
our freedom only by losing it—
    such nakedness, and such clothes!—
leathers "treated" to be tractable
as silk and velvet supplanted by
    aniline facsimile,
shades of medieval shades louder
than the flaunts of Florence!   Our neighbors
    add themselves to the straggling
file we stand in, parti-colored lives
clustered, strung-out, singular, alone,
    these burghers of L.A., some
eager to sample what is promised them,
others uncertain why they have come—
    not turning back but turning
aside, as if reluctant to face
engagements they suspect are lying
    in wait for them up ahead,
although disinclined to loiter long
over an obstacle in their path,
    avoided and already
behind them: *The Burghers of Calais,*

such more-than-life-size Others looming
monochrome and lame, naked
bronze which has gained a life of its own
—green and grisly, but a life of sorts—
by merely being outside. . .

We are safe here; you feel safe, don't you?
for all the sudden menace of a sky
variable to the point
where no one evidently knows how
to be prepared for what is in store. . .
Well, no one alive: *they* know,
the Six made over to their ruin
by Rodin, who a hundred years back
(before there was a museum
in Pasadena) found them waiting
for him in the chronicles of his
fellow snob and countryman
Froissart, recorded without favor
or much fear (five hundred years before
there was a Pasadena),
men who brought themselves to break the siege,
"stripped, barefoot, ready for the hangman":
1)   Jean d'Aire offering the keys
which drag his muscles down to string,
ecstatic as he moves, Calais saved,
to a death an hour away;
2)   Andreu d'Andres encircling his despair
within both arms as if the body
were the pain it knows will come;
3)   Jacques de Wiessant striding, neck oustretched
to let his eyes see *how* it will come
before the lean flesh can learn;
4)   his brother Pierre beckoning—to what?—

under his crooked elbow he looks
     back to find the angry stars
knotted into new constellations;
5)   Eustache de Saint-Pierre wearing the rope
     as though it might prevent him
from falling before he falls for good
and God, huge hands already hanging
     open, helpless, curled to find
comfort in their own unreadiness;
and to complete the invisible
     cube sealing them together,
6)   Jean de Fiennes spreading his arms to let
rags that must once have been finery
     fall open to manifest
a nakedness fiercely young again. . .

Yes, they know what is in store, six men
     shambling to the English camp
where the English queen will save them all,
though they do not yet know about that.
     And maybe they are with us,
always with us, lining up—maybe
we deserve a share of what they know
     and don't know. . . Take any six:
1)   the tall man, for instance, in tight jeans
and a ginger turtleneck, the one
     cupping his hands in order
to look straight into the museum—
is he discovering that to be
     bewitched is not to be saved?
2) Does the black girl—the one behind him
in unforgivable (and unforgiving)
     cerise stretch-pants know we live
as ruins among ruins, rendered lovely
by staring at ourselves in the glass?

5

3)   One man encased in plastic
has turned around to face the statues,
buttoning his coat against the wind—
        does he guess what he appears
to know: where all is bad it must be
4+5)   good to bless the worst? And the two
        who move so much like ourselves—
do they know what we know: that the great
pleasure in life is doing what people say
        you cannot do? At the end
6)   comes a fat woman with a tattoo
on her left wrist—I hear her sighing:
        "God, You have appointed me
from the first day to fall at the feet
of the living and to stand at the head
        of the dying. . ."

                Do they come
like this to their reprieve? Will there be
at the end a forgiveness ready?
        Rodin himself could not show,
how can *I* tell these six the good news:
"You have been chosen, you will be spared"—
        I am standing first in line.

Cats and dogs out there any minute. . .
and in here, now and forever, death
        of a kind, as if a man
needed a diamond and was given
the moon: desire is a relic here,
        Venus becomes a document;
or to put it still another way,
inches of Vermeer can mortify
        massacres by Delacroix
and acres of subsequent carnage
(only the Dealer Takes All), so that

even before we get in,
futility bears down on fatigue
in irresponsible foyers where
    a man can know everything
but nothing else. The omnivorous
package waits, and our riches blind us
    to our poverty. . .

            Bundle up
against the weather and wait your turn;
we are standing where the burial-
    places of our memory
give up their dead. MUSEUM OPEN
SUNDAY UNTIL FIVE. ADMISSION FREE.

On Hearing Your Lover Is Going to the Baths Tonight

Does it matter? Do you mind?
Here, now, is an opportunity for Mind
over Matter, the one triumph: whatever
        in life we really accept
undergoes a change, the world is not the same—
        a quality is added,
        everything has its shadow.
As for *minding*, now's your chance: what easier
        occasion for opening
letters (not those from you) like so many wounds,
finding literal motives for being left
        in the lurch. . . what *is* a lurch?
Before you start spying for real, consider
        what is wrong here, or who wronged?
        Name one man (you included)
whose venery, given vent, has failed to be
        venereal in bringing
home the old surrealist bacon: tireless
pursuit of the Same New Thing! What do you have
        to complain about? Having
things your own way is not really having them:
        jealousy is out, as Proust
        has taken some pains to prove.
It has nothing to do with love, jealousy,
        it is only passed around
at the same time, like pepper with the melon,
for people who happen not to know better:
        anyone who knows melon
would never touch it. Your fantasy of his

body doing what it does
with yours, only doing so
with others. . . is *that* the difficulty? Then
put yourself at ease: two mouths
have never drunk twice from the same chimera.
What he does with you is you; with others, them:
"he" remains a mystery—
you personify only what you are not,
and you are not there. Be glad;
that is a world diminished to an often-
catalogued repository of objects,
possessing no absolute
and final face, no recognitions. There is
(Keats has the words) no wonder
but the human face. What is
that face except our body trying to be
more naked than the body?
Where better than in the dripping faceless dark
for him to discover, and discard, himself,
returning then, rinsed free. . .
All the terminations belong to others,
time alone is yours. Alone.

(I I)

HOMAGE TO NADAR (II)

Eugène Delacroix

The trouble was, you lived in time. That afforded
    a painter no apportioned
place, no purchase; the desert came to nothing.

    Yearly in your features those
of a not to be acknowledged father grew
      unmistakeable until

all ardor darkened, as in your Grand Machines,
    from bitumen and siccatives.
"You must always spoil a picture a little

    in order to finish it"—
and by now you were finished and spoiled as well.
    One diversion never failed:

feeding-time at the Paris Zoo, the tigers
    you resembled (even more
than likely Talleyrand), the destroyers' life-force

    you labelled "le possible"
and prized over what survives. Like Baudelaire,
    your best prophet, you despised

caged hopes, crass progress. Why should you hide your hands
    that had so often produced
what he called *the emphatic truth of gesture*

in life's great circumstances?
Progress past Raphael? You were the first to use
        photographs—for the poses

of "Attila and his Hordes Annihilating
        the Culture of Italy",
fussing like any dandy over your health

        in overheated studios;
and once you left your haughty effigy here,
        you got from Corot the names

of three models: Madame Hirsch, Adèle Rosenfeld
        and Rosine Gompel ("thin arms"),
before you went home and shut yourself up

        for good in the Place Furstenberg,
dying, the Goncourts said, like a dog in his hole.
        Serving time, what was the past

but a burden? The desert would have to serve you
        until there was no more time. . .
"For God's sake," you wrote Nadar, "destroy the plate!"

Jean-François Millet

It was a specialty of yours to divert
    with bedroom vistas—backsides,
breasts, and the bistre provinces between—

    tastes you preferred to beguile
by illustrating, as you so often proposed,
    Fenimore Coopère. Why not?

None of it was real—only art, only Paris,
    that Babylon you traded
for Barbizon, that Paradise, to hallow

    (or create) the *danse macabre*
of Harvest, grim reapers encaged by a row
    of trees that are "like people

who don't speak the same language." We no longer
    speak yours, as you seem to guess,
a goatish corpulence glaring past Nadar

    and this prosperous moment
to a future overtaken by Van Gogh
    and Dali, the ultimate

parody of labor intimately known
    and bitterly resented.
Too biblical to be a Socialist, you kept

    a housemaid in Barbizon
and applied month after month for State handouts:
    not doctrine, convenience

sufficed (the Theories are worse than the Furies)
    to perpetrate a magic
the magician does not expect to fool us,

    though Whitman loved "the sublime
murk" of your empty landscape. What made it myth
    was a classicism invoked

only to show absence and the obstinate
    ugliness of tired bodies. . .
A century separates the sour pastoral:

    you die, and today we prize
some dozen studies for derided images
    turned to gravy. Contempt

is reckless, for what we might have connived
    to attack as a fortress
we are conned into admiring as a ruin.

Jean-Baptiste Camille Corot

For this likeness you forked over one of those
        inevitably silver,
ineffably silly landscapes: *coryphèes*

        passed off as nymphs in forests
composed of feathers, the fraudulent scenery
        of all future *Les Sylphides.*

And in return you posed, a giant, for Nadar
        whose goblin labors managed
to perpetuate here, towering under him,

        your taut half-smile, behind which
the whipped soul is suspended, wanting to be,
        like the world, deceived. By now

you have forgotten that forty years ago
        you said "nothing should be left
to indecision." Everything is left there,

        an expensive wilderness
of blurred, impassive forgeries, till only
        Venice roused you at the end,

as Rome had at the start, to crystalline laws
        unobserved in your lifetime
by admirers too easily satisfied.

        The Claude-glass in your pocket
reminds us of your fate: *it is of no less
        merit to inaugurate*

*a decadence than to bring matters to some
      apogee.* We had supposed
your Second-Empire reveries of false dawns

      and frayed sunsets no more than
études of a cynical science, the hoax
      and hokum of l'Arcadie

du Salon, but sometimes you let us see more:
      any rendering of light
(as Nadar, heaven help us! must have known)

      owes its value to the fact
(not the fiction Gautier called "the inferno
      of ideal weather") that

it is the expression of love. To which end
      you wrote once in your hatband,
"it is logical to begin with the sky. . ."

Giuseppe Verdi

for William Weaver

You are a survivor, even in Paris
    where only success survives,
although its ruins have an eternity

    of their own. Shining ruins,
let that be success, then: *Don Carlos*. And if
    yours was disreputable—

Gautier to the Goncourts: "When the words are sad
    then the music goes *tron tron,*
When the words are happy, then it goes *tra tra*"—

    after all, Wagner fell too,
Jockeyed off the stage just a lustrum ago
    as "Richard Gare de Lyon!"

You do better these days at La Grande Boutique,
    your name for the burgeoning
Palais Garnier; only the French dare call you

    insincere—we don't accuse
oysters of insincerity for making
    their disease into a pearl.

A moment is all you will concede Nadar
    between scenes (in every sense)
at the petty palace, but a moment is all

    he takes to leave this homage
to the perishable clay. In Paris, in *France,*
    a genius is a man who says

what everyone knows, and you speak otherwise
　　to the general ear, with all
the furtive inflexibility of style—

　　Carlos, a sort of dismal
grit in the grandeur, will show them, will make them
　　hear. That is what success means:

being heard, and you have written how many
　　bad operas to write the good,
how many good to write the great ones to come,

　　luminous, voluminous,
voices wrapped in the gift each sex possesses
　　of not listening to the other.

We listen to you and applaud not because
　　we believe you (we do not),
we applaud you for making life credible.

Giacomo Meyerbeer

Poise was always your pose, Jakob; not just here
    in the staring studio
(where at seventy you flaunt the guarded peace

    of those who have ceased to ask
what comes next—for Jakob, it appears *you know*!),
    but in the Opera House

(where a society gets—and disavows—
    the sorcery it deserves).
Poise was your profession from the first; perhaps

    you had it when Clementi
pushed you, barely seven, on stage in Berlin
    to perform the D minor

Concerto of another prodigy who died
    the year you were born; or when
the Singspiel you wrote for von Weber failed

    and Salieri (in Vienna)
cautioned against composing "too Viennese":
    one hand washes the other

till all hands are clean. . . To Venice then you came
    where Rossini's cauldron seethed
about your ears, and the music fell between

    all stools—or into them, as
that demented Wagner keeps saying. You have heard
    better "Jewish jokes" than his

these forty-five years—just now you told Nadar
    your favorite: who was it
gave Palestine its name? The Philistines!

    "We Jews are always German
at puberty, but we die French." Three more years
    and you will die frank, at least:

"composing operas without my old Scribe
    is like having to grow up
over and over—an eternal process

    of learning what can't be done
well, or again, or ever." You wanted fame
    on your own terms or no fame—

no hollow victories. And you had just that,
    poised conjuror, had your cold
and commonplace legerdemain. Hold the pose.

Hector Berlioz

How much can a man lose of what he has had
before the losses begin
to alter what he is? Job's question, and just

the one you must answer now:
Harriet drunk and estranged; the childhood friend
whom you married *faute de pire*

paralyzed, her eyelashes making a noise
like a bat on the pillow,
inert as that second half of *Les Troyens*

postponed beyond all patience
and drastically cut, a ringing blunder
last Monday at the Lyrique;

your boy, complaining of tunes *inside his head*
—where else, you smiled, should they be?—
like a pat of butter melted from your life. . .

How many years had Austria
applauded, Russia and even England paid
to hail what Paris ignored?

Yet here you loom, another apparent heir
to the whole century's myth:
was genius no more than some Grand Manner

of preparing the tinder?
Your phoenix played its incendiary part
with too manifest a faith

in its ashes, your serpent devoured its tail
 with a decided languor.
Nowadays you read only the Comedies,

  Romeo no longer; *Lear*
had music in it, none of which was yours:
 "Shakespeare can be forgiven

anything but ourselves." *Life,* you told Nadar
 as you thrust your bitten nails
into those kindly all-concealing sleeves, *life*

  is enough to cure anyone
of the romantic delusion that there is
 something lordly. in disorder.

Out of the casserole, *cher maître, maître chef,*
 and into the empty pit?
Let there be silence—and there was. Long silence.

Jules Michelet

You would not let him include your Anaïs
    —*épouse en secondes noces,*
a nymph as yet unnoticeably pregnant—

    in this scowling effigy:
"to look like a national monument *and*
    its custodian—never!"

By now your face makes only bones about it:
    you suspect the worst, which is
simply what happens, a figured bass whereon

    to develop progressions.
"Progress" of course was a progress toward
    disaster, and it had come

to this for you—telling a story regains
    the meaning it must have had
for Scheherazade: postponing the future.

    "In that case," your child-wife put
a child's question during the pose, "why bother
    studying what has been lost?"

"So you may be one of those who remember
    what it was, my dear. There is
no past to speak of, other than such defeats. . .

    Our talent to record
has much more to do with forgetting than with
    remembering—with keeping

the past in the past rather than creating
    the past new in the present.
Having 'a sense of history' does not mean

    I have *written* history,
nor believing in progress mean I believe
    any progress has been made."

Bugs, birds, sex, and the sea will henceforth sustain
    your inquiry (the Greek word
for *history*, after all). Let the rest go,

    the kings and the priests; no more
Lamentations! All you can see now comes to
    Apocalypse—this is how

the world looks when the ego disappears. Only
    when we know nothing is new
can we live as if it all might become new.

Gérard de Nerval

taken a week before the poet's suicide

She began coming to him on summer nights,
    and even that first time
he knew there would be more—not because she was

    Balkis (whispering the name),
Queen of Sheba, but because he knew himself
    to be Solomon, and wise:

she needed him! Like starlight she lay, radiant. . .
    "Her hair is soft, Théophile,
and her voice so beautiful you will never

    understand a word she says."
This he explained as he trembled back to truth;
    "I see in the world only

what already lives in my mind, but to see
    what inhabits his own mind,
a man needs the world." Théophile understood:

    "Gérard, you must get her back. . ."
And into the East he vanished, for like all
    preternaturally real

persons, his movements were those of a ghost—
    Lebanon, Egypt—Sheba!
and just as mysteriously reappeared. . .

He had lost her—*he* was lost.
"Gérard, how did she look?" "Tiny hands and feet
and a smile like a scalpel!"

So eager was he to possess—he was made
so happy by any sign
of her fidelity—that he must have felt

something like pleasure even
in a regularly recurring fever. . .
They found him black in the face,

strangled by a corset-string he used to say
was Mme de Maintenon's:
he would take it out of his shirt and show it

at parties. He was hanging
from a rail in the Rue de la Vieille Lanterne,
"tenebrous, widowed, unconsoled."

The air is no more than ink now—in Paris
all midsummer nights are dreams.
Her hair was softer than starlight, and as bright.

Anatole France

Your name meant a row of red books, properly
    voluminous although not
Anatolian, as far as I could determine:

    I was nine when I found them,
serried on a low shelf where I could ponder
    the mysterious titles;

Penguin Island sounded promising, of course,
    but Mother, who had mastered
any number, favored the tale of Thaïs—

    at her wedding (the first one)
she recalled that the violinist had played, she reminisced,
    the "meditation" from *Thaïs*. . .

That was the Midwest, and the 1930's—
    you had been done in, long since,
by the Paris of your *belle époque* triumphs,

    and if Mother was grateful
for glimpses vouchsafed into the Grand Salon
    and your *cabinet de travail*,

it had already dawned on Valéry, on Gide
    —for Breton it was high noon—
that there were no other rooms in your villa,

    no closet in which a crime
could be committed, no alcove, no plumbing!
    Not that your name draws a blank—

how could it, parading the patriotic
      pseudonym which would become
a synonym for your limitations. Nadar's

      medallion does you justice,
a version that need not chip, crack or tarnish:
      sharp and detailed and dead wrong.

You could not see the Strange, hindered by strangeness,
      and your recognition of
the Familiar was foiled by familiarity.

      Decades back, the long red row
disappeared, for when we can no longer change
      the world, the world changes us.

You scoffed at Rodin for "collaborating
      too closely with catastrophe"—
Success was your mode. You have not been pardoned.

(III)

On *Lately Looking into Chapman's*
Jane Austen:
A Critical Bibliography

"The passions," Charlotte Bronte was at pains
to notify her correspondent (male),
"are perfectly unknown to her. Of course
a lady! all you like—I see you do—

but as a woman, incomplete." "She is
unpleasant—English in the snobbish sense:
a mean old maid," wrote Lady Chatterly's
creator, and the list goes on from there.

Can we forgive her? Even Henry James
was likely to be snappish on the score
of "our dear, their dear, everybody's dear
Aunt Jane. . ." who had never trifled with Keats

and travelled not at all in "realms of gold"
or any other glamour, if we trust
her answer (after *Emma!*) to the Prince,
that she confined herself to "pictures of

domestic life in country villages,
and could no more engage to write Romance
than Epic Poems!" Keats, who could, affords
a clue. Consult *our* Chapman (anything

but "loud and bold"—amazingly discreet),
and feel instead "like a watcher of the . . . *depths*
when a new *species* swims into his ken":
for her—for the species Austen—love, like death,

is the great leveller, but not because
everyone loves (or dies), but just because
no one—not even Lawrence—understands
what love (or death) can mean. And we are left,

eagle-eyed or even a little dim,
to ogle each other "with a wild surmise,
silent on a pique" (ah, Charlotte!), still
commanded to acknowledge what *she* knows:

that Wisdom's secret is detachment, not
withdrawal. And that nobody is damned
except by his own deliberate act. Or hers. . .
Perfectly unknown? "If we have not lived

within a family, we cannot well say
what any of its members' griefs may be";
holding her method by that end, she pulled,
and as she pulled, it came. Homeric Jane.

Carrion (continued)

DEAR CHARLES,
              if I may: have there not ensued
between us correspondences enough
to warrant such familiarity?

I know your destestation of Device—
how you hated all contraptions (but rhyme)
and explicity determined *la vraie*

civilisation n'est pas dans le gaz
ni la vapeur, mais dans la diminution
des traces du péché originel. . . Yet

by mere mechanism has been discovered
a perspective you would have said cut down
the prospects of the sin you called 'original',

though that is a bad dream I cannot share
—after all, you went to some pains to prove
the real is what we can awaken from.

Charles, a means has been found of making time
accelerate within a lens and then
upon a screen, whereby the world can see

"the thing *you* saw that lovely summer day":
carrion, rot incarnate, charnel (all
the words that put death in any body!),

some animal—senseless expression for
what spread, no longer animate, upon
a clump of compost in some vague terrain,

an empty lot which made it plain: the plot
thins. There lay putrescence, an easy or
—who knows?—an eager prey (it would appear

absence of power absolutely corrupts)
to the host of maggots you were the first
poet to apostrophize: vermin, hence verse!

and frenzied creatures with consuming speed
chewed their way through time condensed by light
to change the corpus of mortality

(the whole is always vaguer than its parts)
into an accurate shackle of bones.
Still, not one maggot struck out on its own—

as if destruction had no preference
to show, as if diminishment could come
only at once, en masse, a legion doom!

Blurring the infiltrated eyes and ears,
then filing the mouth to a thorough fare,
mysteriously they seethed together

before scaling mountainous shoulders and
a belly where, in seconds, who could say
what was ravenous and what ravine? You,

Charles, whose only sensuality
was to be in pain, you would have divined
how the post- must feed on the pre-

and how, in the beautiful process served
according to these engines' evidence,
we are blessed by our deprivations, if

we let ourselves be. Easing what had been
an opus into an operation, look!
the matter lasted, by these lights, at most

a minute, and what kept the worms at one
and the same task, what made their taskmaster,
said the voice-over, out of the microphone,

was a digestive liquor grubs exude
as grubs exert, substantially eye to
eye, so that each assumes it eats the next,

and all these absorbing devotions do in
the dead thing left undone by its own life.
This was revealed by what is called *time-lapse*

photography, which gives our living-room
the languor of an opium parlor—shows
the same blue glow you would have recognized,

Charles, but it was only *television*!
the one expression banned by Eliot
(your surest advocate among the shades

in death's great city) who declared the word
unmete or at least unmetrical for verse.
Say it *was* gas and steam, then, which tell (or

televise) the truth I *can* share with you,
not to correct but to confirm your joy,
the poetry of casting off life's chains . . .

Watching that carrion consumed, I knew:
what devours us, how paltry it is; but what
we are devoured by—ah, Charles, how great!

Homage

There's a Ford in your future
But the Ford in your past
Is the Ford you have now
So you better make it last.

ADVERTISING JINGLE,

CIRCA 1946

Mid-August, the mid-twenties,
writing from Guermantes—I saw the French postmark;
you could have made it up, of course, another
    of your fat, nourishing fibs,
but there they were, Proust's own "orange" syllables
incontrovertible on the envelope
    (some truth is close to being
only a consistent lie, as we shall learn
when the last of your memorialists dies off)—
    you more or less volunteered
for the obsessional task which lures me still:
"it would amuse me to translate *Swann*." Ever
    the good soldier ("I somehow
pine to publish a volume of poems before
the war ends or I am killed"), you knew
    the way the saddest story
ought to go, leading us (not only Marcel)
slowly back down from the heights, following some
    path of blithe declivity—
the reason for a mistress. Proust escaped you:
now you would have to produce, as all of us
    long to do, a great dreary
masterpiece everyone must claim to have read;
it was either happiness or art. By then
    you had invented yourself

49

under (or over) the emblematic name,
bringing out your fiftieth book and the first
    novel by "Ford Madox Ford";
losing a father, gaining a fatherland
in that neat reversal, repudiating
    his tainted Teutonism
(though Provence was "in the family" for good)
for a new-made man, *homo scriptor,* to whom
    literature and fiction
were different, irreconcilable dooms,
literature being a luxury and
    fiction a necessity.
"I have for facts a most profound contempt," though
after dozens of books and two daughters, sighing
    "I do wish I had a son,"
enmeshed from divorce to divorce by a strong
if sleepy sexuality which somehow
    worked against the grain of love
(what was saucy in the gander, I daresay,
was not saucy in the goose). Meanwhile you ditched
    your legacy, the dry glare
of pre-Raphaelite masters *and* the wet mist
of Impressionism, steeping yourself instead—
    "to discover where we stand"—
in that inclusive negative, the Modern:
"but for Conrad, who told me 'put more shadow
    in it, there *is* more shadow,'
I should be merely a continuation
of Dante Gabriel Rossetti." Which is
    what it has been my study
to continue, if headway can be something
besides continual parricide, eager
    to commit poetic acts
between consenting adults and managing
to ravel a sow's purse out of that silk ear. . .

You smile at my ambition,
you forbid nothing, suggesting only—do
I hear you?—that poems, even your poems,
        be labelled, like medicines:
Shake Well Before Using. How you got away
from them—from "Aunt Christina" and the others
        was your great exploit, how you
survived originality, whereas I. . .
I go round on the back of that other life
        my reading relinquishes
like the little Egyptian heron that lives
on the backs of cows. The shoe fits perfectly.
        There is no getting beyond
without first getting as far, you remind me,
part "denture", part "danger", the self-proclaimed
        model for James's Merton
as he (HJ, not Densher) was yours in all
but success: "I am a half-way house between
        the unpublishable young
and real money, a sort of green-baize swing-door
to kick on entering and leaving, both ways."
        Well, who has got beyond *you*,
who wants to? I cannot bear to imagine
your last years—did it *have* to be Michigan,
        when all America seemed
like a blue-point oyster, very large, very
insipid? You wanted countries built out of
        obstacles and boundaries,
like Guermantes, say—the fields that resemble
a dinner-table one has just left, gardens
        gently warding off darkness
with red flowers. . . I leave you there, confronting
"with a certain erudition most of the things
        which make for the happiness
of mankind," the shadows deepening, the light

orange as Proust said it sounded: *Guermantes*. . .
Just light enough to read by,
reading what? Joyce, or Yeats, who died your last year?
No, some new writer not even printed yet,
formal as the familiar
rapturous sentences in the first lessons
of a French primer: *il aime, il écrit, il meurt.*

Impersonations

for Paul Schmidt

I *Portrait of Pierre Loti* by Henri Rousseau, 1906
   (KUNSTHAUS, ZURICH)

> Serenely frontal, sharing with his cat
> a concentration we may not deserve
> but must endure, the novelist at gaze
> in semi-Oriental garb (tarboosh
> and scarlet tunic skewered by one pearl
> beneath a quite Parisian collar) is
> smoking—like a chimney, as we say,
>
> and not surprisingly, a mile behind
> his elbow smokes a chimney, one of four
> the size of that candescent cigarette.
> Enrich these correspondences to read
> corner to corner: fingers then offset
> the factory stacks, acacias match the cat,
> and lo! such clever symmetries set off
>
> a fact impossible to miss—Pierre Loti
> is missing one ear! as if to manifest
> the message of an earnest Decadence:
> every artist, however "balanced", must
> sever someone's ear and serve it up
> for the world to shout into—the human ear,
> that whirlpool wild to draw Creation in. . .
>
> Peering deep into appearances,
> the Abyssinian is tame and drawn
> with both ears iridescent, being so
> intent on secret tidings—*sacré chat!*
> whereby is conjured up (inferences from
> Egypt are a favorite with Rousseau)
> cults of Bubastis, the mysterious East. . .

How well such Levantine allusions work
or play upon our sympathies, our sense
that Fiction's levity is quite as fraught
with duty as the weight of History;
deftest of all, the Douanier's device
of having his luminary turn a cold
shoulder on the mills of Saint-Germain,

ignoring doggedly (or cattily?)
urban evacuation just the way
the Lady in the Louvre, propped against
a livid wilderness, unmakes *her* scene:
how properly then he orients Loti,
who patiently made his pitch to literature
as the Thousand-and-One Evenings of the West.

What is more European, after all,
than to be corrupted by the Orient?
Yet just when we are readiest to learn—
O pâle débauche—from this pseudonymous
letch that the body's inertia is a part
of the body's force, our lesson is forestalled. . .
Enter Scholarship, eager to report:

*Sitter unknown to painter and to Art
History*, whose attributions are
hastily revised to accommodate
this copy of a portrait of Someone Else,
Monsieur Quelconque in the 1906 Salon,
later acknowledged to be rather "like"
Pierre Loti—that nose, those eyes, why not?

As recognizeable as the (retired)
Captain Viaud in his villa near Hendaye
marshalling Asian regalia for the next
fancy-dress Parisian party, while
"Pierre Loti" in yet more gorgeous drag—
embroidered palms and parrots, gold on green,
the uniform of *l'Académie-Française*—

is inducted under its Dome, and the real Loti,
hero of all those yellow and yellowing books
habitual to "gentle readers", lies
—lies!—romantically dead, decades ago,
under crumbling Constantinopolitan walls.
Then who on earth or in hell is this? Our name,
if it does not name us, reminds us of our name. . .

Loti survives or supersedes "Loti",
palmes académiques and Damascan palms
in a golden haze of indistinct surprise,
the Villa Stamboul's naughty souvenirs
which make each mantelpiece a minor *souk*—
survives it all because he was not born
to be saved but born to be pleased! A fugitive

for whom the only shelter possible
was a shining Elsewhere, and who wrote it down
to put off the future, like Scheherazade,
insisting he could substitute the self
for mere *sagesse*. Osiris makes the point
which he would prove: real life always begins
with resurrection, even in this world.

II   *Loti Costumed as Osiris*, photograph by Montastier, 1906
    (MUSÉE CARNAVALET, PARIS)

The throne he sat in must have barged right through
the throng of Tuesday regulars *chez* Madame
Adam. What a name! and, looking round
at the other masqueraders, what a set!
although attendance here—as Monsieur Eve?—
might seat him by a comfortable vote
on one of the Immortal Forty's chairs. . .

The which, if he could trust her promises,
would be a seemly throne, and a way as well
of taking his revenge on Mallarmé's
still-rankling Tuesdays in the Rue de Rome
(to *those* soirées he never had been asked,
and wondered still what the old fraud and his friends
were up to? Whatever it was, who needed them? . . .).

Assume then that *this* throne was carried in,
sprouting ivory lotuses everywhere—
as if the very name they knew him by
were a sly allusion to the plural form—
and carefully lowered by his *fellahin*
to a stage conspiratorially set
before the revellers arrived: *voilà*!

he carried it off, for all the whispering
of envious Célimènes and Mélisandes
(new, these last, this season). . . Look how well
the leopard-skin embellishes his waist
and how he holds the lopped-off cypress staff
which signifies the Scattered God's rebirth,
and in the other hand that Lalique orb

(no doubt a flagon from Madame's boudoir) —
these are the attributes of an aplomb
not to be shaken: Loti is divine,
though the Uraeus signifying so
—asp and solar disc whose silver rays
emanate from an earlier *roi soleil*—
trembles slightly on the firm-fleshed brow. . .

Resurrection! but first comes the death
and diaspora of all that must die:
in Loti's case, the thing has happened twice—
as a man, then as a writer. Never old
enough to be young again, he would decline
into that savagery of circumstance
where language is so rapidly transformed

each generation fails to understand
what the one before was saying. . . Did he sit
motionless throughout the revelry,
posing and deposing (both at once)
that love is desire for knowledge, and desire
always an impulse toward archaic forms,
the locus of an impossible Return?

The party's over, and this ludicrous
figure, preserved in two albumen prints
(one with no Uraeus but a Flail—
to symbolize, perhaps, less mastery
than the sacred scourge of such futilities
as Madame Adam's bygone *bal masqué*),
is not a total loss but a legacy:

the world he "rendered" was a magic gift
bestowed by a roving victim, yet became
rent and rendered in another sense,
eroded to such thin consistency
by time (as each world of the flesh must be)
that ever and again the giver's name
drops into darkness, one more flash

in the Pantheon of our deluded hopes. . .
We are the heirs of this careful charlatan
for whom only the Vague was dangerous,
life without adjectives. . . death to him.
Better in your failures to be new
than old in your success, plausible,
possible, plastic—anything but dim!

Fabulous yet real, an epiphany
gleams from book to book, right to the last,
Fleurs d'Ennui. Now *that* was nerve, to tag
the evil gardener with your catalogue
of precious names, pathetic images. . .
Between your Asiatic spells, the brain's
abracadabra and the body's algebra,

lodges your message: we shall be entire
only by acknowledging ourselves
(like torn Osiris) in dismemberment!
Let Egypt's trappings exorcise the God
who would not get the joke (gods never do):
age cannot wither nor the *douanier*
steal your infinite identity.

At the Monument to Pierre Louÿs

Jardin du Luxembourg

Sage nor Saint nor Soldier—these were not
the sobriquets he fastened onto Fame:
let other men indulge the mummery
endorsed by these obsequious thoroughfares

with such abandon, yard by gravelled yard—
theirs would not be the idols he adored.
What *were* the sacred semblances he chose
to traffic in? And did they cheat his trust?

Inchmeal moss has muddled the design:
a palm? a laurel? or an aureole
as futile as anathemas would be?
The cenotaph *his own estate* bequeathed

(as though forewarned no Popular Demand
would pay a sculptor, specify a plot
and meet the tariff of Perpetual Care)—
the cenotaph! obtrusive as it is,

thwarts all my efforts at decipherment.
Just as well. There is no cause to mind
whatever mutilations have occurred
as though in nothing solider than mud,

to mourn what the successive rain has made
of this "immutable" monstrosity
erected to an undermined career
beginning only when—as History does—

the tale it has to tell attains its end.
Appropriate decay: like "other men"
he lived in search of what he saw as joy,
ecstatic consolations. *There she stands!*

Balancing an urn as effortlessly
as if no more than his very ashes swelled
its brimming load, behind the stele looms
an academic Naiad rather worse

for wear but rising (the intent is clear)
gently from the reeds' enjambment—she
is cold but she is patient, waiting for
the furtive metal of her eyes to fill. . .

Glancing back in haste to catechize
her shoulders where they falter, suddenly.
she catches up a hank of molten hair
and wrings it out as if it had become

another green, wet, heavy nenuphar:
she waits for the tune of little drops to fall. . .
Also appropriate: what else remains
of him but *l'odeur de la femme,* page after page?

And even that would soon evaporate
without the fickle traces of three friends
(Valéry desisted, Gide despised,
Debussy meant what he said but managed to die)

—save for such captious cameraderies,
nothing would survive a period taste
but this absurd contraption: brazen Muse
and marble slab on which all syllables

erode but APHRODITE BILITIS—
the rest is. . . silly. Who was Pierre Louÿs?
The real names of the poems in his books,
for all their happy Sapphic hoaxes, are

. . . *and Other Poems*. Night after night he wrote
as if there were a tide to float him on,
nacre enough to laminate his itch—
who was it called him an oyster inside a pearl?

If once and for all he could make chance into choice,
change what he had to love to what he wanted to. . .
Forever hostage to the chiding animal,
he was elided. In his will was no

peace, as he learned whenever a meal came late
or the nearest pissotière was occupied:
the change never ceases, never being complete.
There *is* a tide in the affairs of men,

but apt to strand them high and dry. You haunt
my frequentations of your great
contemporaries like a thirsty ghost. . .
I read you, *mon semblable, mon Pierre!*

Attic Red-Figure Calyx, Revelling in Progress, circa 510 B.C.

Attributed to Zagros; Z-6, iii,
collection University of Texas, Austin

It makes sense now, at least our senses make it,
that we should sort together here, in our so
        promiscuous conjunctions
which point, perhaps, to the fear of being cut
off: diagnosing us, you would have to go
        farther back than to the womb—
go, in fact, all the way back to the penis. . .
It means *telling apart*, diagnosis:
        "the stubborn center must be
scattered," Shelley says, yet we abide, untold.
Almost any time, that summer, you could glance
        into the big glass above
the bar and find some of the six of us—Ken,
Leagros, Larry and Panaitios,
        Scott, Hieron: the love-names
vary with the vase-painter's propensity—
marionettes rehearsing crucifixion!
        each on a cross of his own,
each fallen because he does not realize,
however vertical a man may be here,
        however erect he must,
that a Fall has occurred. When I invoke "here"
I refer to this repeatedly ravished
        and quite as often retouched
Greek pot which happens to be the name as well
of our favorite backroom bar, THE GREEK POTHOLE.
        "Now" is then, and "here" is there:
Noon. South. In each wave the sun and a seaworm,
in each lump of earth a centipede hugging
        the day's core as for dear life.

I speak from that bar in Texas opening
wide as a myth, uttered by the mouth and not
    the thing done, the work performed:
mythos not *ergon* speaks, whether from Naxos
or Texas. For I speak too from that mended
    calyx around whose axis
we move, just one damned thing after another,
red figures gleeful against their ground. *Figures*
    speak, that is the assumption:
we receive our riches only when they come
to meet us on another's voice. The Greek pot
    and THE GREEK POTHOLE are one.
The last thing you get to know is what comes first:
members of a circle in a square world, we spend
    ourselves in mirrors, and not
knowing where to begin is our beginning. . .
Let Ken open his cloak, the folds disclosing
    boldly, baldly, a belly
drawn smooth with a comprehensible volume—
we feel we know what is on the other side.
    Dim and lank and limp and dank,
his tiny genitals grant no inkling of
what Ken, as we all know, can make of himself
    on occasion. By the way
we touch one another, even when we shake
the fingers off, we assert our permanent
    need to live by the pattern
rather than by the fact. When Larry raises
the two-handled cup he stumbles and falters,
    but Scott, goatish, vigilant,
catches him before a drop can be wasted.
Without a bush to hedge with, Scott stands out,
    every hair by this light
incandescent, even his sandy beard burns,
and the cup does not fall. Larry drinks again.
    At this moment all creatures

become flaming creatures, as if they had
just been turned into the shape they share: it is
        a dance, not a diagram,
by which we indulge the young more than the old—
because they are young, not because they are right.
        We choose one another, chase
around the edges what changes with our choice:
only when there are differences between
        one moment and another
of pleasure can we go on being happy
with the same person—*heresy*, remember,
        is the Greek word for choosing:
Ken lives in hell and likes it; Larry runs
past, his day a color and his night a sport;
        Scott entertains a downward
appetite to mix with mud. . . Surely ours is
a longing once held to be impossible
        and now inevitable,
the craving to create what is there and not
merely to contemplate it. Yet the beauty
        of our dance, each limb lapping
its neighbor, comes from our spanning, our holding
together an empty space, the darkness in there
        making our orbit brighter
outside; for this vessel of our is a shrine
with an undisturbed absence at the center
        of which we may never speak,
though we observe, like the hours for time. Consult us,
red, vivid, mutable, and you can never
        lose sight of the void we frame.

(I V)

HELLENISTICS

Ithaca: The Palace at Four a.m.

for Katha Pollitt

FIRST WORDS

No god could make up for the ten years lost
(except by ten years found). Nor would I dream
of trying anything so grandiose
my first night home. Was I trying at all?
Hard to say, when it has taken this long
to be in a fitting position. . . Still,

your old responses seemed to be intact
before I even touched you. Wasn't it good?
For me it was: all that I waited for
(and I did wait, you know—those episodes
with silly what's-her-name were meaningless)
ever since we left those invincible walls

smoking behind us, the islands, the sea
between. . . But if you had been satisfied,
would you have left me sleeping behind you?
Not of course that *I* could satisfy you,
but the occasion itself? Surely that
afforded a fulfillment sleep might crown!

Just look around you: not one trace of blood
left on the marble, not a sign there was
anything like a massacre downstairs
only yesterday morning; then dinner—
wasn't that a nice dinner they gave us?
as if they served a banquet every night!

But all of that—or none of it—would do:
the house swept clean of the scum you condoned
(I won't say encouraged, but they did hang on!)
and things back where habit said they belonged:
your own husband lying in your own bed. . .
Yet you had to leave it! Without showing

much solicitude for a light sleeper
who might, after all, have been easily
disturbed (straw rustles and an old bed creaks,
you know: I've grown accustomed to keeping
my ears open—wandering will do that),
you seemed to *drift* over to that corner

where you always kept your loom—it's still there!
and with only one clay lamp to see by
set. . . to work? Penelope, I am here.
You don't have to do whatever it was
you told them you were doing any more—
stop picking at that thing, come back to me!

LAST WORDS

What I "have to do" has nothing to do
with what I have—or with doing, either.
You tell me I have you. Evidently
you can't imagine what it means to live
inside a legend—scratch a Hero and
you're likely to find almost anything!

Having scratched, I found you. Was I surprised?
Once her womb becomes a cave of the winds
which appears to be uninhabited,
there are no surprises for a woman—
she has survived them all. But at the loom
I learned that even you were ignorant,

crafty Ulysses! Weaving taught me: our
makeshifts become our mode until there is
no such thing as *meanwhile*. Not craft but art!
So you see, I must ravel the design
all over again: there is no end in sight.
Ulysses home? You don't come home at all,

wandering will do that, though I say it
who never left. The loom's my odyssey—
dare I call it my penelopiad?
You think you were asleep just now, don't you,
after those homecoming exertions? But
you were never here at all, my husband:

the sea still has you—I heard you insist
you were No-one. No one? How many times
you sighed 'Circe' in that light sleep of yours:
she must have had her points, old what's-her-name.
You snored but sirens sang, and when the moon
silvered our bed you seemed to feel the sun

depositing tiny crystals of salt
all over your old skin. You were away.
That was your weaving—and my wandering.
The suitors are dead, your bow is a prop,
but neither of *us* is present. Let me
give you some peace at this ungodly hour. . .

Be patient—having found or feigned this much,
perhaps the two of us can fool the world
into seeing that famous genre scene:
The King and Queen Restored. It's abstinence
that makes the heart meander: you're at sea,
I worry this web. Lover, welcome home!

Cygnus cygnus *to Leda*

for Mona Van Duyn

While that charlatan strutted and preened, I watched
      from the bushes: both of you
   seemed unconcerned, visibly detached.

No need of a bird's eye view to see, my dear—
      whether you were done yourself,
   the tryst was at an end. Now listen. . .

Listening, actually, would have made clear
      just what was up between you
   in such preternatural silence—

didn't you suspect *something* in all that ease
      and efficiency—as if
   even swans could do it on the wing?

The word *means* "sound", you silly goose, it follows
      from *swan* there must be *singing*!
   You might have known from the noiselessness—

you should have guessed: he was a decoy, only
      some god and not one of us!
   In our world, no matter how willing

(I *saw* the kind of resistance you displayed)
      girls can no longer "converse
   with animal forms of wisdom night

and day"; there must be preparation, doings
     and undoings—otherwise
   you get the Seducer you deserve:

a quack! If all it takes is *feathers* to make
     a fine friend somewhat fonder,
   how would you react (rapturously,

am I wrong?) to a strident suitor who comes
     to you not in fancy dress
   but as the Real Thing? Any human

can make History, it's easy as laying
     an egg! Don't you want to be
   more than a god's way of creating

another god? Look into your heart and confess
     the hope (the fear?) of otherness:
   take me and get *out* of history!

Joy, Leda—joy requires more surrender, more
     courage than pain: surrender
   to joy and serve the unknown darkness!

Here in the merciful air that is without
     a shape it chooses to keep,
   some particle of chaos can be yours

beneath the unregarding stars. Lie down now.
     Troy is no progeniture
   worth your having, once its heroes lose

their little immortality. Limbs are no dance!
     Even stones possess a love—
   a love that seeks the ground. Look at me!

Cygnus cygnus *to Leda*

It's no affair of mine to save you, Leda,
        but to make you worth saving,
    being lost. It's in you: I can hear

    the SWAN. Swan-song. All fates are "worse than death".
        Leda, I offer you all
    except to be human or a god!

Narcissus Explains

In Memory of David Osborne

Any number of stories are told
      (mostly tedious sermons
      on Vanity. If you ask me,
         where there's an image
      there's hope—without an idol
      in it, what's a heaven for?)
and any number of theories spawned
      from the dawn of time until
      this afternoon—endeavors
         by the inventive
      to decipher the reasons
      I loiter here, perched on my
riverbank, pondering the features
      which incessantly reform
      under my gaze (reforms
         are Nature's *forte*,
      as I have found—if She has
      one weakness, it's that She can't
do Her thing just once. Rivers resume. . .),
      although some sources assert
      it is no more than a pond,
         barely a freshet
      which fastens my attention
      so fast to myself: "the springs
of Narcissism," they say, "are shallow."

And of course there is Freud's myth of me
      which proposes that I act
      (if you can call it acting—
         let's say I *behave*)

as if I were my mother
"and thus enjoy being loved"—
this is Freud—"by myself." Note that *thus*!
Mums, you know, is a minor
Naiad named Leriope,
madly *dégagée*
about the consequences
of a dip in my father—
you may have heard of him: Cephesus?
He passes, in Boeotia,
for a torrent. Anyway,
according to Freud,
I love myself-as-a-boy
because (now get this) I "tend
to identify with the parent
at whose hands I have suffered
the more severe frustrations."
Need I remind you,
Daddy has *no hands at all*,
and Leriope is far
too silly to frustrate anyone!
I say, we love not only ourselves
but what ourselves can become:
best to keep an eye—keep both!—
on what we *have* loved
if we cultivate fond hopes
of there being any future
in it. That's what I'm doing right now
where the river serves my turn,
my academy, my rule. . .
It is religion,
this belief that *whatever
happens to me must matter*,
and can never, for just that reason,
altogether disappear
from the world. Body dearest,

all I have is you,
you and the water that knows
forever the things of once. . .
Have I so much? My darling flesh,
even the loveliest of
mortals can make love to no
more than what you are:
the shroud or is it the shrine
dividing us—bodily—
from what we call our divinity?

No, the tale's truth is to be defined
elsewhere. To be found, in fact,
by night, when the dark water
comes into its own;
after sunset you can hear
the solar system laughing
in the stream. I think it laughs in Greek.
Once my pored-over image
is effaced by the longed-for
metamorphosis,
in its place the entire sky
is rife with stars reflected
by unseen water. I wait for night
to become such a glory,
and then I become the night.
Now you understand
why there is no Narcissus
among the stars: I engross
all figures there by my gradual
consideration! I faint
beside the river until
night and the stars fill
my emptiness. I cite your saint
who minted *soliloquy*:
"having found amazement, I found peace."

(V)

Move Still, Still So

for Sanford Friedman

*Now that I am nearly sixty, I venture to do
very unconventional things.*   LEWIS CARROLL

1925

. . . bothers me, Doctor, more than the rest,
> more than anything
> I've told you so far—
anything, that is, I could tell you.
> You see, I have this
> feeling, actually
a need. . . I don't know what to call it—yes,
> that's right, *tendency*:
> you know what I mean,
you always know, I suppose that's why
> I'm here at all or
> why I keep coming
back to you when nothing ever seems
> to change. . . I have this
> "tendency" to lie
perfectly still when he wants me to
> let him inside me,
> all of a sudden
I turn passive—how I hate that word!
> I mean I don't feel
> anything is wrong,
but it always happens, just before. . .
> I suppose nothing
> private is really
shocking, so long as it remains yours,
> but I wish I knew
> if other women

felt this way. I mean, it seems as if
    once he's in there I'm
    waiting for something.
The stillness bothers me. Why can't I
    accept it? Not what
    he's doing there, but
the stillness: I can't bear it. Why is that?

1895

> *And was it my fault*
> *it rained Gladyses*
> *and globes? Quite right of Mrs Grundy,*
> *sending you to bed*
> *one whole day before*
> *your usual time, and since you broke*
> *the window, making*
> *you mend it yourself*
> *with a needle and thread. . . Now, Gladys,*
> *don't fidget so much,*
> *listen to what I say;*
> *I know ways of fixing a restless*
> *child for photographs:*
> *I wedge her, standing,*
> *into the corner of a room, or*
> *if she's lying down,*
> *into the angle*
> *of a sofa. Gladys child, look here*
> *into the lens, and*
> *I'll tell you something. . .*

All these years, Doctor, and I never
    knew: was I having
    it or wasn't I?
What I thought I was supposed to have

wasn't what *he* thought
I should be having,
and to this day I don't think he knows,
or any man knows—
do *you* know, Doctor?
Does it matter if you know or not?
How could a man know—
how or even when
a woman has such things for herself.
Men all imagine
it's the same as theirs,
and of course they think there's only one. . .

. . .*No you're not. Boredom
is something inside
people, not anything from outside.
To borrow a word
from Mrs Grundy,
there must be a knot tied in the thread
before we can sew.
Your pose is my knot,
and this camera my way to sew. . .
Did you ever see
a needle so huge?
Of course, having such a thing at home
is preposterous:
it is by having
preposterous possessions that one can
keep them at arm's length. . .*

Before it happens
I don't move, almost not breathing at all,
and I think it's *that*,
the lack of response
he gets discouraged by. He thinks I'm
dead. I wouldn't mind

> letting on, Doctor,
but if it happens I just can't speak—
> I can't even move.
> He thinks it happens
only when I pretend it happens. . .

> > *Now that I've made friends*
> > *with a real Princess,*
> > *I don't intend ever to speak to*
> > *any more children*
> > *who haven't titles;*
> > *but perhaps you have a title, dear,*
> > *and you don't know it.*
> > *I'm cantankerous,*
> > *but not about that sort of thing—about*
> > *cooking and grammar*
> > *and dresses and dogs. . .*

Sometimes I pretend—to save his pride
> and prevent a row.
> It seems politer,
that way: why be rude about such things?

> > *Now try it a few*
> > *minutes like that, child.*
> > *Lovely, lovely—one hardly sees why*
> > *this little princess*
> > *should ever need be*
> > *covered up by dreadful crinolines.*
> > *Much better that way.*
> > *Princess Perdita,*
> > *have I told you about her, Gladys?*
> > *the one in the* Tale
> > *from Shakespeare, who thought*
> > *she was a shepherdess, when in fact*

she was a real live
princess all the time!

It can happen, and it does, without
tremendous effort,
but unless I take
control and make it the way I want,
it won't work at all. . .
At a certain point
I have to stop trying to fool him
and focus all my
forces on myself.
There must be a feeling that the waves
will come to a crest
—higher waves. Doctor,
sometimes it seems like too much trouble. . .

When the prince saw her—
not doing anything,
just being herself, singing a song
and dancing a bit
at the sheep-shearing,
you know what he told her? Now listen!
What you do, *he said,*
not even guessing
she was a princess, and Perdita
not knowing either,
still betters what is done. When you speak
I'd have you do it ever, when you sing
I'd have you buy and sell so, so give alms,
and for the ordering of your affairs,
to sing them too. When you do dance, I wish you
a wave of the sea, that you might ever do
nothing but that, move still, still so,
and own no other function. . .

Of course it's entirely personal—
          there's no way to share
          what happens to me,
but I like it that he's there. I always
          want to keep my eyes
          open, I do try
to make myself feel that much closer
          to him, but meanwhile
          all I'm conscious of—
the only thing, to tell the truth, is
          my own pleasure. There!
          That time I said it,
my own pleasure: that is what it is!

          And you'll see, Gladys,
          that's what photographs
          can do, make you a wave of the sea
          that you might ever
          do nothing but that. . .
          So very soon the child-face is gone
          forever, sometimes
          it is not even
          there in children—*hired models are*
          plebeian, they. have
          thick ankles and tend
          to be heavy, which I cannot admire.
          And of course I must
          have little girls, you know
          I do not admire naked little boys
          in pictures—they seem
          to need clothes, always,
          whereas one hardly sees why the forms
          of little girls should
          ever be covered.

I can't make it happen without the right
               imagining. Sometimes
               I can't bring it off
and I cast around in my mind for
               proper images—
               rather improper,
I'm afraid. I may manage to keep
               high and dry by day
               but with the last light
I venture into the water, all
               that white froth fainting
               out into darkness—
as if the world had become one wave. . .

        Stockings, even these
        lovely ones, seem to me
        such a pity when a child like you has
        (as is not always
        the case) well-shaped calves.
        Yes, that's it. I think we might venture
        to face Mrs Grundy
        to the extent of
        making a fairy's clothes transparent?
        I think Mrs G
        might be fairly well
        content to find a fairy dressed at all. . .

        I know it isn't
        supposed to matter,
but whoever said it wasn't so
        important for women
        must have been a man!

There we are, ready. Now Gladys, dear,
I want you to lie
still, perfectly still.
I'll help you do it, but the impulse
must be your own. Three
minutes of perfect
stillness will do for both you and me. . .

I always feel cheated whenever
                    it happens to him
                    and not to me too.
I treasure those glimpses of the waves
                    and the high white foam.
                    I am suspended
before they fall. Doctor, what happens
                    in that one moment
                    of timeless suspense?
I feel cast up, out of life, held there
                    and then down, broken
                    on the rocks, tossed back,
part of the ebb and the flow. Doctor,
                    would you mind if I
                    just lay here, quite still
for a moment? Just this one time, still. . .